Poetry for Cats

Poetry for Cats

The Definitive Anthology of
Distinguished Feline Verse

By

Henry Beard

Illustrations by
Gary Zamchick

A John Boswell Associates Book

VILLARD BOOKS
New York
1994

For Serafina
il miglior gatto

Contents

Poetry
for Cats

Grendel's Dog, from BEOCAT

by the Old English Epic's Unknown Author's Cat*

Brave Beocat,   brood-kit of Ecgthmeow,
Hearth-pet of Hrothgar   in whose high halls
He mauled without mercy   many fat mice,
Night did not find napping   nor snack-feasting.
The wary war-cat,   whiskered paw-wielder,
Bearer of the burnished neck-belt,   gold-braided collar band,
Feller of fleas   fatal, too, to ticks,
The work of wonder-smiths,   woven with witches' charms,
Sat on the throne-seat   his ears like sword-points
Upraised, sharp-tipped,   listening for peril-sounds,
When he heard from the moor-hill   howls of the hell-hound,
Gruesome hunger-grunts   of Grendel's Great Dane,
Deadly doom-mutt,   dread demon-dog.
Then boasted Beocat,   noble battle-kitten,
Bane of barrow-bunnies,   bold seeker of nest-booty:
"If hand of man unhasped   the heavy hall-door
And freed me to frolic forth   to fight the fang-bearing fiend,
I would lay the whelpling low   with lethal claw-blows;
Fur would fly   and the foe would taste death-food.
But resounding snooze-noise,   stern slumber-thunder,
Nose-music of men snoring   mead-hammered in the wine-hall,
Fills me with sorrow-feeling   for Fate does not see fit
To send some fingered folk   to lift the firm-fastened latch
That I might go grapple   with the grim ghoul-pooch."
Thus spoke the mouse-shredder,   hunter of hall-pests,
Short-haired Hrodent-slayer,   greatest of the pussy-Geats.

*Modern English verse translation by the Editor's Cat.

The Cat's Tale

by Geoffrey Chaucer's Cat

A Cat there was, a gentil taillees Manx
Our Hoste hadde seen astray on Thames banks
And taken home to ridden him of rats,
At whiche she preved to been the beste of cats.
He longed to bringe on pilgrimage his pette,
But Puss bigan to fussen and to frette
When that she sawgh the leathern hond-luggage
In whiche she was yschlept when on viage;
She thinketh that no Canterbury mous
Be worth an expeditioun from hir hous,
And so she took hir leave of us apace
And crept into a secret hiding-place,
And when the folk the pavement gan to pounde,
This Pussie-Cat was nowhere to be founde,
And she was leften in the hostelrye
To keepen all the rodentes compaignye;
And that is how this Cat withouten tail
Became as wel a Cat withouten tale.

Helen's Cat, from MEPHISTOPHELES, OR THE TRAGICAL HISTORY OF DOCTOR FAUSTUS'S CAT

by Christopher Marlowe's Cat

Was this the puss that munched a thousand mice
And napped atop the towers of Ilium?
Sweet cat, your kiss will give me nine more lives!
Her purr doth make a furball of my soul:
See where it issues from my gaping mouth!
Come, kitten, come, give me my soul again.
Here will I dwell, and for a kiss from thee
I will despoil the stately halls of Troy,
Smash painted urns to bits with wanton paws,
And slash to ribands costly tapestries,
For in thy shining whiskers heaven lies,
And all are dogs that are not Helen's cat.

Hamlet's Cat's Soliloquy,
from HAMLET'S CAT

by William Shakespeare's Cat

To go outside, and there perchance to stay
Or to remain within: that is the question:
Whether 'tis better for a cat to suffer
The cuffs and buffets of inclement weather
That Nature rains on those who roam abroad,
Or take a nap upon a scrap of carpet,
And so by dozing melt the solid hours
That clog the clock's bright gears with sullen time
And stall the dinner bell. To sit, to stare
Outdoors, and by a stare to seem to state
A wish to venture forth without delay,
Then when the portal's opened up, to stand
As if transfixed by doubt. To prowl; to sleep;
To choose not knowing when we may once more
Our readmittance gain: aye, there's the hairball;
For if a paw were shaped to turn a knob,
Or work a lock or slip a window-catch,
And going out and coming in were made
As simple as the breaking of a bowl,
What cat would bear the household's petty plagues,
The cook's well-practiced kicks, the butler's broom,
The infant's careless pokes, the tickled ears,
The trampled tail, and all the daily shocks
That fur is heir to, when, of his own will,
He might his exodus or entrance make

With a mere mitten? Who would spaniels fear,
Or strays trespassing from a neighbor's yard,
But that the dread of our unheeded cries
And scratches at a barricaded door
No claw can open up, dispels our nerve
And makes us rather bear our humans' faults
Than run away to unguessed miseries?
Thus caution doth make house cats of us all;
And thus the bristling hair of resolution
Is softened up with the pale brush of thought,
And since our choices hinge on weighty things,
We pause upon the threshold of decision.

Vet, Be Not Proud

by John Donne's Cat

Vet, be not proud, though thou canst make cats die
Thou livest but one life, while we live nine,
And if our lives were half as bleak as thine,
We would not seek from thy cold grasp to fly.
We do not slave our daily bread to buy;
Our eyes are blind to gold and silver's shine;
We owe no debt, we pay no tax or fine;
We tremble not when creditors draw nigh.
The sickest animal that thou dost treat
Is weller than a man; in peace we dwell
And know not guilt or sin, and fear not hell:
Poor vet, we live in heaven at thy feet.
But do not think that any cat will weep
When thee a Higher Vet doth put to sleep.

To the Kittens,
to Make Much of Time

by Robert Herrick's Cat

Get ye a human while ye may,
   When you are still a kitten,
For by a cat too long a stray
   Men's hearts are seldom smitten.

The master of yon cozy house
   May wed a maid with puppies;
Or set a trap to catch that mouse,
   Or buy a bowl of guppies.

Cold rains will soon the summer drown,
   And ice will crack the willow;
And though the snow is soft as down,
   It makes a chilly pillow.

Then hands that would have stroked your head,
   When you came in from prowling,
Will hurl at you a boot instead
   To halt your awful howling.

The Prologue to TERRITORY LOST

by John Milton's Cat

Of cats' first disobedience, and the height
Of that forbidden tree whose doom'd ascent
Brought man into the world to help us down
And made us subject to his moods and whims,
For though we may have knock'd an apple loose
As we were carried safely to the ground,
We never said to eat th'accursed thing,
But yet with him were exiled from our place
With loss of hosts of sweet celestial mice
And toothsome baby birds of paradise,
And so were sent to stray across the earth
And suffer dogs, until some greater Cat
Restore us, and regain the blissful yard,
Sing, Heavenly Mews, that on the ancient banks
Of Egypt's sacred river didst inspire
That pharaoh who first taught the sons of men
To worship members of our feline breed:
Instruct me in th'unfolding of my tale;
Make fast my grasp upon my theme's dark threads
That undistracted save by naps and snacks
I may o'ercome our native reticence
And justify the ways of cats to men.

The Mongrel

by William Blake's Cat

Mongrel! Mongrel! Barking blight,
Bane upon my yard at night;
What infernal hand or eye,
Could frame thy vile anatomy?

In what stagnant sump or pool
Steep'd the slobber of thy drool?
What the wrath dare he incur?
What the hand dare weave thy fur?

Who the crackpot, who the nut
Would wish to make an ugly mutt?
And when thy heart began to tick,
What weird hand withheld the brick?

Where's the crank who loos'd thy chain?
From what peapod came thy brain?
What warp'd artist shaped thy face?
Whose foul crime the canine race?

When the cats gave up their prowls,
And cowered from the hellhound's howls:
Did he smile his work to see?
Did he who made the Flea make thee?

Mongrel! Mongrel! Barking blight,
Bane upon my yard at night;
What infernal hand or eye,
Could frame thy vile anatomy?

Cottontails

by William Wordsworth's Cat

I wandered hungry as a hawk
That floats on high o'er hills and dales,
When all at once I stopped to stalk
A clutch of little cottontails;
Beside the lake, among the reeds,
Quavering and squealing in the weeds.

As featherbrained as the bugs that land
And dally in my dinner bowl,
They clung together in a band
Around the bottom of a hole:
A dozen saw I at a glance,
Frozen with fear in terror's trance.

And though they did not dance or play
But simply sat and stared at me,
A kitten could not be but gay,
In such delicious company:
I ate—and ate—the whole sweet pack.
Oh, what a tasty rabbit snack!

And oft, when on my couch I lie
In vacant or in pensive mood,
They flash upon that inward eye
That conjures up a favorite food;
And then into a ball I scrunch,
And dream about that bunny lunch.

Kubla Kat

by Samuel Taylor Coleridge's Cat

In Xanadu did Kubla Kat
A splendid sofa-bed decree
With silken cushions soft and fat
A perfect feline habitat
   Set on a gilt settee.
And twice ten yards of fine brocade
The golden ottoman arrayed:
And there were pillows packed with airy down
Hand-plucked from sacred swans in Thessaly;
And lace draped from a massive silver crown
Adorned the ornate rosewood canopy.

And ah! that seat effused a potent lotion
Pressed from the leaves of rare hypnotic herbs
Sweet source of wondrous dreams that naught disturbs.
Oh magic mint! Sublime and blissful potion!
   The fragrance of that place of slumber
   Floated on the balmy breeze
   Drawing kittens without number:
   Persians, Manx, and Siamese.
It was a miracle of opulence,
A shining sofa-bed with catnip scents!

A songbird with a small guitar
In a vision I once did note:
It was a wise and winsome owl,
A sweet and elegant fowl,
Sitting in a pea-green boat,
Singing a song to me,
And hand in hand, on the edge of the sand,
We danced by the light of the moon.

And when I arose from my languorous swoon
I built that divine divan,
That cushy couch! that smell of spice!
And all who saw should stop and yawn,
And none would cry, Get down! Begone!
The lights are dimmed, the curtains drawn.
Tiptoe round him, still as mice,
And let him catnap on his bed,
For he on catnip leaves has fed,
And lapped the milk of Paradise.

She Walks in Booties

by George Gordon, Lord Byron's Cat

She walks in booties, like a sprite
   With pixie feet and fairy toes;
Her paws on ice will ne'er alight
   Nor feel the chill of frigid snows;
And all the rays of winter's light
   Shine on her collar's satin bows.

And from her soft enchanted fur
   Exudes the scent of sweet shampoo
And precious oils distilled from myrrh
   That give her hair its magic hue:
I long to hear her charming purr,
   And share the music of her mew.

But as I watch her take the air,
   My spellbound vision starts to fade;
I feel at once a dark despair;
   My feline heart is sore dismay'd;
For not content to make her fair,
   Her doting owners had her spay'd!

Abyssinias

by Percy Bysshe Shelley's Cat

I met a traveler from an antique land
Who said: A huge four-footed limestone form
Sits in the desert, sinking in the sand.
Its whiskered face, though marred by wind and storm,
Still flaunts the dainty ears, the collar band
And feline traits the sculptor well portrayed:
The bearing of a born aristocrat,
The stubborn will no mortal can dissuade.
And on its base, in long-dead alphabets,
These words are set: "Reward for missing cat!
His name is Abyssinias, pet of pets;
I, Ozymandias, will a fortune pay
For his return. He heard me speak of vets—
O foolish King! And so he ran away."

On First Looking into Clarke's Larder

by John Keats's Cat

Much have I traveled with the poet Keats,
　　And many shabby homes and mansions seen;
　　'Neath many meager tables have I been,
But never did I spy such scanty eats,
As when he went to hear Homeric feats
　　Read by a friend of his named Clarke, a dean.
　　My supper was a single small sardine,
And so I went to loot the larder's treats.
I ope'd the pantry doors with noiseless paws,
　　And lines of hare and squab and pheasant scanned;
Then felt I like a lion whose swift claws
　　Bring down some beast, and soon, too gorged to stand,
He sits and tears the carcass with his jaws,
　　Silent, upon a plain in Swaziland.

To a Vase

by Elizabeth Barrett Browning's Cat

How do I break thee? Let me count the ways.
I break thee if thou art at any height
My paw can reach, when, smarting from some slight,
I sulk, or have one of my crazy days.
I break thee with an accidental graze
Or twitch of tail, if I should take a fright.
I break thee out of pure and simple spite
The way I broke the jar of mayonnaise.
I break thee if a bug upon thee sits.
I break thee if I'm in a playful mood,
And then I wrestle with the shiny bits.
I break thee if I do not like my food.
And if someone thy shards together fits,
I'll break thee once again when thou art glued.

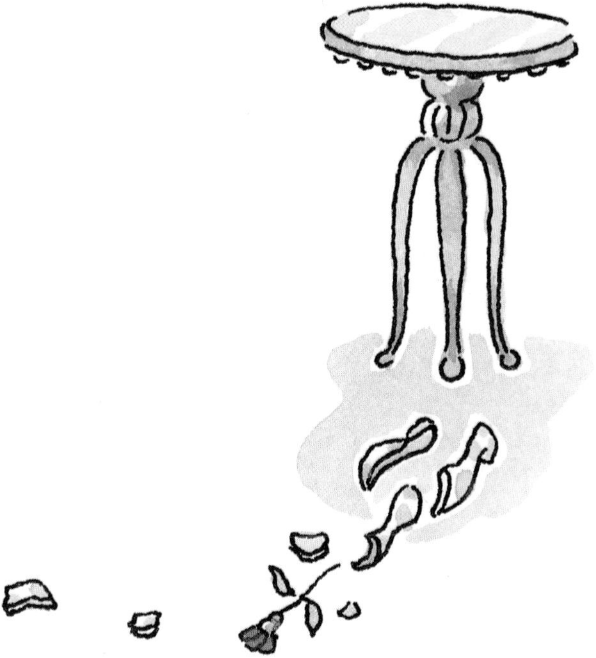

The Hairball and the Mouse

by Henry Wadsworth Longfellow's Cat

I chased a mouse beneath the stair,
It went to ground, I knew not where;
For, so swiftly it ran, my sight
Could not follow it in its flight.

I coughed a hairball in the air,
It fell to earth, I knew not where;
For though my sight is sharp and true,
I saw not where that fur-bullet flew.

Some time afterward, quite by chance,
I spied them both in a single glance;
For the mouse in a corner lay dead,
A hairball lodged in his tiny head.

The End of the Raven

by Edgar Allan Poe's Cat

On a night quite unenchanting, when the rain was downward slanting,
I awakened to the ranting of the man I catch mice for.
Tipsy and a bit unshaven, in a tone I found quite craven,
Poe was talking to a Raven perched above the chamber door.
"Raven's very tasty," thought I, as I tiptoed o'er the floor,
          "There is nothing I like more."

Soft upon the rug I treaded, calm and careful as I headed
Toward his roost atop that dreaded bust of Pallas I deplore.
While the bard and birdie chattered, I made sure that nothing clattered,
Creaked, or snapped, or fell, or shattered, as I crossed the corridor;
For his house is crammed with trinkets, curios and weird decor—
          Bric-a-brac and junk galore.

Still the Raven never fluttered, standing stock-still as he uttered,
In a voice that shrieked and sputtered, his two cents' worth—
                                        "Nevermore."
While this dirge the birdbrain kept up, oh, so silently I crept up,
Then I crouched and quickly leapt up, pouncing on the feathered bore.
Soon he was a heap of plumage, and a little blood and gore—
          Only this and not much more.

"Oooo!" my pickled poet cried out, "Pussycat, it's time I dried out!
Never sat I in my hideout talking to a bird before;
How I've wallowed in self-pity, while my gallant, valiant kitty
Put an end to that damned ditty"—then I heard him start to snore.
Back atop the door I clambered, eyed that statue I abhor,
        Jumped—and smashed it on the floor.

Cleaning the Box

by Alfred, Lord Tennyson's Cat

Cat-turds on parquet blocks
    Are one clear sign for thee!
'Tis time to do the cleaning of the box
    Which you put out for me.

For while to you my litter seems pristine,
    To me it plainly reeks
Like stinking bilges in some barkentine
    Becalmed for weeks.

Twilight and evening bell,
    And after that the dark!
And there shall be no inkling of farewell,
    When I embark.

And though you call for me with plaintive cries
    That echo from the rocks,
You will not see your cat materialize,
    'Til you have cleaned my box.

Mousing at Night

by Robert Browning's Cat

The moon-lit fields and the smell of loam;
And the soft brown soil beneath my paws;
And the startled little mice that jump
From their nest inside a leafy clump,
As I kill my prey with sharpened claws,
And pick it up and head for home.

Then a mile or so along the street
'Til the house stands out against the sky;
A whine at the door, a quick sharp scratch,
The bright blue flash of a lighted match,
Then a muffled curse, and a strangled cry,
As I drop the corpse by slippered feet.

Meow of Myself, from LEAVES OF CATNIP

by Walt Whitman's Cat

1

I situate myself, and seat myself,
And where you recline I shall recline,
For every armchair belonging to you as good as belongs to me.

I loaf and curl up my tail,
I yawn and loaf at my ease after rolling in the catnip patch.

My tongue, every fiber of my fur, form'd from this soil, this
    mole that lives in this soil,
Born here of native cats born here from native cats the same,
    and their sires and dams the same,
I, now seven years old in perfect health begin,
Hoping never to see a vet.

2

Who naps there? rummaging, sly, whimsical, cute;
How is it I extract strength from the mice I eat?

What is a cat anyhow? why am I one? why aren't you?

All you mark as your own I shall take as my own,
Else what is the point of having me around.

I do not grovel the way dogs grovel the world over,
Nose-down digging up bones and fetching the flung stick.

Whimpering and whining to be taken for a walk, longing for
    the leash, bred to come to heel for a hundred generations;
I wear my flea collar as I please indoors or out.

Why should I beg? why should I do tricks? why should I
    capitulate and be obsequious?

Having pawed through closets, snoop'd beneath the stair,
    ransack'd the drawers and open'd every carton,
I find no finer stuff than the fur that grows on my own body.

3

Kosmos, a tabby, of Walt Whitman the cat,
Corpulent, hairy, playful, sleeping, snacking, and rambling,
No exhibitionist, no show-off around men and women or
    apart from them,
No more tamed than untamed.

Throw open the doors and hook them to the walls!
Install cat-doors in the walls themselves!

Whoever declaws another declaws me,
And whatever is done in pet hospitals is offensive to me.

Through me the furballs rising and rising, through me the
    detritus of meals long past.

I utter the cat-sound primeval, I give the meow of the
    democratic kitty,
I bathe in America's copious dust,
I sip cool water from her flowerpots and toilet bowls.

I lick myself, there is a lot of me and all so luscious,
Each mealtime and whatever happens to drop from the dinner
    table fills me with joy,
I cannot tell what my instincts know, nor whence the source
    of my deepest urge,
Nor the cause of the impulse to gallop off, nor the cause of
    the impulse to gallop back again.

Behold the day-break!
I awaken you by sitting on your chest and purring in your face,
I stir you with muscular paw-prods, I rouse you with toe-bites,
Walt, you have slept enough, why don't you get up?

4

I believe that a leaf of catnip is no less than the birthright
    of a kitten,

And a June bug is equally welcome, and a buzzing fly, and the
chick of the wren,
And the chipmunk is an hors d'oeuvre for the highest,
And the running bunny would belong on a table in heaven,
And the wriggling rodent in my paw puts to shame all restaurants,
And the shrew crunched between my jaws surpasses any banquet,
And a mouse is a greater miracle than anything that touches the
palates of quintillions of gastronomes.

I find I assimilate yarn, beads, pieces of string, rubber bands,
paper clips, house plants,
And am spackl'd with bits of chewed mammals and bird-babes
all over,
And have consumed what is put before me for any reason,
But cough anything back up again when I desire it.

In vain the sudden dash or subterfuge,
In vain the nervous squirrels scatter nuts at my passing,
In vain the field mouse retreats beneath the procreating mulch,
In vain breakable objects steady themselves and assume different
shapes,
In vain the fishpond stilling its surface and the giant carp
hunkering down in the depths,
In vain the moth flutters against the window screen,
In vain the hamster wheels faster and faster in its axel'd cage,
In vain the gerbil takes to the inner corners of its box,
In vain the songbird seeks his sanctuary in the sycamore,

I follow quickly, I ascend to the nest in the highest crook of
the tree.

5

Listener down there! why do you hide from me?
Look up at my face while I bellow in the baffles of evening,
(Talk promptly, no one else hears me, and I do not want to spend
the night up here.)

Do I make a nuisance of myself?
Very well then I make a nuisance of myself,
(I am a cat, I possess an attitude.)

I ululate toward him who should draw nigh, I wait on the tree-limb.

Has he done his day's work? when is supper?
Who wishes to play with me?

Will you speak before I go berserk? why are you so late?

6

The noisy jay swoops by and reviles me, he complains of my meow
and my malingering.

I too am not a bit subdued, I too am uncontrollable,
I sound my splenetic yowl over the roof of the house.

The last clouds of day draw back,
They part, and one final shaft of light casts my long shadow
  on the lawn below,
It reminds me how far I am from the ground.

I sniff the cooling air, I twitch my whiskers at the setting sun,
I shiver as the wind riffles my fur into fluffy waves.

I berate myself for the climb that took me from the grass I love,
If you want me again look for me above your hat-brim.

You can never know where I am or what I am,
But I am good company to you nonetheless,
And really do regret I broke your inkwell.

Failing to find me at first keep looking,
Missing me one place search another,
I sit up here waiting for you to come and carry me down.

Dover Sole

by Matthew Arnold's Cat

The sea smells sweet to-night,
The tide is low, the soft waves roll
Along the beach;—on the French coast, a light
Gleams, and is gone; let's hope some tipsy Frog
Ran down a poodle. From the tranquil bay
Comes the distant tang of fresh-caught sole!
Only, below in the waterway,
Battered prows part the wisps of fog,
Listen! you hear the deep-toned toll
Of buoy-bells which the boats' wakes rock, and ring,
As they return and tightly clog
The little port, and then the men begin
The slow unloading of the catch, and bring
The delicious scent of supper in.

Epicurus's cat long ago
Smelled it on the Aegean, and it brought
Into his mind a just-deboned turbot
Unguarded in the kitchen; he
Could well have been the father of the thought
That something's to be said for gluttony.

The smell of fish
Grows stronger still, and on the kitchen stair
A box of neat fillets sits packed with ice.
And now I clearly hear
The monger's wagon rattling through the square,
Delivering the dinner dish
From the seafood shop down by the iron pier.
Farewell to thoughts of dreary mice!

Ah, fish, there is no fare
Quite like a flounder! They surely will not miss
A piece or two from stacks of sole like this;
I'll steal a few, but leave the lion's share.
Look! the lamplight on the lane is pretty;
They're back from walking out on Dover Beach.
I think I'll hide and spare myself the speech,
For we are in a world untouched by pity
Where ignorant humans curse the kitty.

There Is No Cat-toy Like a Mouse

by Emily Dickinson's Cat

There is no Cat-toy like a Mouse
To please me in my Play
Nor any Yarn-ball like a Bug
That strains to fly away—

No rubber Bauble can delight
No lifeless String divert—
For where is Fun if none feels Fright
Or Joy if nothing's hurt?

Pawed Ugliness

by Gerard Manley Hopkins's Cat

Damn dogs and every draggled doggy thing—
   Fang-spangled spaniels with slaver-slovened flews;
    Gangle-lanky Afghans, funny in the head;
Slack bassets; smug pugs; Spot, Fido, Rover, King;
   Whatever buries, harries, chases, fetches, chews;
    All dogs lap-, bird-, watch-, guide-, sheep-, show-, sled-;
Hocks, hackles, withers, stifles, brisket, ruff;
   Loud hounds or snuffling puppies (who knows whose?)
    Mangy mongrel mix, snoot-snouted purebred;
And all who boister forth to strut their mutty stuff:
                      Drop dead.

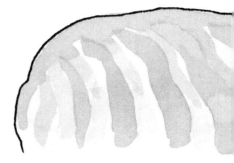

From A CAT'S GARDEN OF VERSES

by Robert Louis Stevenson's Cat

The Rain

The rain is raining all around,
  It rains on me and you;
I hope the neighbor's dog has drowned,
  Or caught a fatal flu.

Mealtime

A mousie squealing in a trap
Woke me from my morning nap.
Wasn't he so very sweet
To tell me it was time to eat?

Whole Duty of Cats

A cat should never kill a mouse
Until he's chased it through the house,
And shown it to another kitten,
Before its little head is bitten.

Catty Thought

The world is so full
    of such edible things,
I'll nibble their feet,
    and I'll chew off their wings.

If—

by Rudyard Kipling's Cat

If you can disappear when all about you
    Are madly searching for you everywhere,
And then just when they start to leave without you,
    Turn up as if you always were right there;
If you can shed your hair in any season,
    And cough up half of all that you devour,
And rush from room to room without a reason,
    Then sit and stare at nothing for an hour;

If you can kill the baby birds that twitter,
    But not the voles that eat bulbs by the score;
If you can scatter heaps of kitty litter,
    Yet still leave droppings strewn across the floor;
If you can tear a precious rug to tatters,
    But keep your scratching post unmarked by claw;
If you can play with china till it shatters,
    But never touch your cat toys with a paw;

If you can try to nap where someone's sitting,
    Although there is another empty chair,
Then rub against his ankle without quitting
    Until he rises from your favorite lair;
If you can whine and whimper by a portal
    Until the bolted door is opened wide,
Then howl as if you've got a wound that's mortal
    Until he comes and lets you back inside;

If you can give a guest a nasty spiking,
    But purr when you are petted by a thief;
If you can find the food not to your liking
    Because they put some cheese in with the beef;
If you can leave no proffered hand unbitten,
    And pay no heed to any rule or ban,
Then all will say you are a Cat, my kitten,
    And—which is more—you'll make a fool of Man!

The Dismal Isle of Innisfree

by William Butler Yeats's Cat

I must arise and hide now, or go to Innisfree,
To the dank hut he built there, of mud and rubbish made:
The only thing you'll find there is about a billion bees,
And mushed-up beans in a soggy glade.

And you get bit by ticks there, for ticks come dropping down,
Dropping from the leaves of the nettles, to lodge within your fur;
There breezes smell of cow-flops, the lake is dirty brown,
And right next door lives a nasty cur.

I will arise and hide now, for any time I see
The box in which I'm carried positioned by the door,
I know it's time to vanish, and to the cellar flee:
My Innisfree beneath the floor.

From CATS ARE KIND

by Stephen Crane's Cat

I saw a dog pursuing automobiles;
On and on he sped.
I was puzzled by this;
I accosted the dog.
"If you catch one," I said,
"What will you do with it?"

"Dumb cat," he cried,
And ran on.

• • •

A man said to the universe,
"Sir, I exist!"
"Excellent," replied the universe,
"I've been looking for someone
To take care of my cats."

Furball

by Gertrude Stein's Cat

Furball is a furball is a furball.

Sitting by the Fire
on a Snowy Evening

by Robert Frost's Cat

Whose chair this is by now I know.
He's somewhere in the forest though;
He will not see me sitting here
A place I'm not supposed to go.

He really is a little queer
To leave his fire's cozy cheer
And ride out by the frozen lake
The coldest evening of the year.

To love the snow it takes a flake:
The chill that makes your footpads ache,
The drifts too high to lurk or creep,
The icicles that drip and break.

His chair is comfy, soft and deep.
But I have got an urge to leap,
And mice to catch before I sleep.
And mice to catch before I sleep.

Thunderstorm

by Carl Sandburg's Cat

The storm comes
on big human feet.

It goes stomping
across harbor and city
in clumsy hipboots
and then plods on.

The Emperor of Tunafish

by Wallace Stevens's Cat

Call the opener of little round tins,
The strong-fingered one, and bid him spill
From kitchen cupboards concatenating cans.
Let the rabbits nibble on fresh greens
As they are wont to do, and let the moles
Dig tunnels in the path of the lawnmower.
Let food be finale of wish.
The only emperor is the emperor of tunafish.

Take from the drawer on slides,
The one where the gadgets are kept, that thing
With which you dismantle metal lids
And twist it so as to remove the top.
Be sure to scrape off all the stew or hash
Before you throw the cover in the trash.
Leave the can beside the dish.
The only emperor is the emperor of tunafish.

The Yellow Goldfish

by William Carlos Williams's Cat

so much depends
upon

a yellow gold
fish

washed down with bowl
water

inside the white
kitten.

In the Window of a Pet Shop

by Ezra Pound's Cat

The apparition of those noses on the glass
Mushrooms on the wet, slick grass.

Treed

by Joyce Kilmer's Cat

I think that I shall never see
A poem nifty as a tree.

A tree whose rugged trunk seems meant
To speed a happy cat's ascent;

A tree that laughs at dogs all day
And serves up baby birds for prey;

A tree whose limbs are in the sky
Where clandestinely I can spy;

Until it does upon me dawn
It is a mile down to the lawn.

Poems are made by cats like me,
But only you can get me off this goddam stupid tree.

The Love Song of J. Morris Housecat

by T. S. Eliot's Cat

M'io muoiano muole miglio miù
miei ma miogni noi parlamiaou
muoi m'uomi miure ne più
miolo muoiano mio siamiaou.

Dante's Cat

Let us roam then, you and I,
When the evening is splayed out across the sky
Like a kitten neutered on a laboratory slab;
Let us stray on paths through neighbors' yards
Behind the boulevards
Where raccoons scuttle in the refuse bins
Scattering cellophane and potato skins:
Paths that follow like a nagging accusation
Of a minor violation
To lead you to the ultimate reproof . . .
Oh, do not say, "Bad kitty!"
Let us go and prowl the city.

In the rooms the cats run to and fro
Auditioning for a Broadway show.

The soft white fog that rises from the rubbish heap,
The soft white cloud that surges through the rubbish heap,
Flows into the corners of the million-dollar set;
The wave of dry-ice smoke that rolls waist-deep
Lathers the human actors' fake-fur suits
As they ham it up to the music's beats,
Forms into pools in the orchestra pit,
And leaves a chemical smell on the front-row seats.

And indeed there will be time
For the soft white smoke that spills along the stage,
Curling in wisps around the rubbish heap;
There will be time, there will be time
To calculate in human years your feline age.
There will be time to wheedle and cajole,
Time to beg the guests who come to tea
To drop leftover tidbits in your bowl;
Time to sniff at a kitchen scrap,
And time yet for some unforeseen obsessions,
And time for new digressions and transgressions,
Before the taking of another nap.

In the rooms the cats run to and fro
Auditioning for a Broadway show.

And indeed there will be time
To wonder, "Do I shed?" and, "Do I shed?"
Time to turn back and stretch out on the bed,
And give myself a bath before I'm fed—
(They will say: "It's the short-haired ones I prefer.")
My flea collar buckled neatly in my fur,
My expression cool and distant but softened by a gentle purr—
(They will say: "I'm allergic to his fur!")
Do I dare
Jump up on the table?
In an instant there is time
For excursions and inversions that will make me seem unstable.

For I have known the ones who feed me, known them all—
Have known my humans well and leaned against their shins,
I have measured out my lives in catfood tins;
I know the voices calling with a singsong call:
But is it dinner, or is it time to hide?
    And should I go outside?

And I have known the hands already, known them all—
The hands that pet you while you try to take a nap,
The brusque insistent thumbs, the fingers lacking in tact,
And when I am kneaded like a bread-dough ball,
Then how should I react?
Should I cough up a furball in your lap?
    Then should I go outside?

And I have known the feet already, known them all—
Feet that are booted or slippered or bare
(And tread upon your tail when you lie along the stair.)
And is it true it rankles
When I rub against your ankles?
Feet that cross beneath the table, or walk along the hall.
    So should I go outside?
    And then demand to come back in?

     . . . . .

Do you know, I have walked along the neat suburban streets
And seen the hand-drawn posters of missing cats
Stapled to the maples where poodles lift their legs? . . .

I should have been two pairs of spotted paws
Padding across a sea of sighing grass.

     . . . . .

And in the afternoon, the evening, I sleep so fitfully,
Tickled by a bony digit,
I sleep . . . but you notice that I fidget.
Stretched out beside you on the old settee,
Should I, after liver snacks and tastes of last night's roast,
Chase a ball or claw my scratching post?
For though I have hissed and growled, hissed and spat,
Though I have brought a mouse (grown slightly cold) and dropped
    it on the landing,
I am no predator—life outdoors is too demanding.
I like a proper dinner and my kitty litter.
I have seen the Infernal Vet inspect my teeth, and titter.
In short, I am a 'fraidy cat.

And would it have been worth it, after all,
Amid the broken cups, the nibbled plants,
Amid the cat hairs on your best grey pants,
Amid the claw marks in the carpet pile,
Would it have been worth my while
To have dropped a half-dead chipmunk in the hall
And left it squirming like a pregnant pause,
As if to say, "I would have purchased you a pocket watch instead,
But as a cat, I lacked the wherewithal"—
Or if sitting on a pillow by your head,
    My look might mean: "I am not sure what I am doing here at all.
    I am an animal, after all."

And would it then be worth while, after all,
Would it then be worth my while,
Amid the splintered chair legs and the lacerated rugs,
Amid the scratches on the banister, amid the shredded drapes that
    frame the terrace door,
Amid the fragments on the floor—
If I could shatter my mystique,
If that bitter yellow fluid from the bottle with the dropper could
    enable me to speak,
Then would it be worth while
If, sitting on the sofa in my customary sprawl,
I should turn in your direction, and remark:
    "I am really not upset at all.
    I just grew tired of my rubber ball."

                    . . . . .

No! I am not a Practical Cat, nor was I meant to be;
I am a household pet—I will suffice
To warm an empty room, dispatch some mice,
Distract you with my play, amuse a guest:
An easy pet to own, a small expense,
Fastidious, a bit inscrutable,
Temperamental, quick to take offense;
At times, indeed, wholly unsuitable—
Almost, at times, a pest.

I grow fat . . . I grow fat . . .
I shall wear white woolen booties and a silly hat.

Shall I have my fur shampooed? Do I dare to eat some quiche?
I shall wear a little jacket and walk upon a leash.
I will never knock the knickknacks from their niche.

I do not think they'll have me put to sleep.

I have seen the tomcats in the vacant lots
Parading through the ash piles in a pack
With their tails hooked high and their ears bent back.

We will gather on a fuming rubbish heap
And prowl the musty alleys of a slum
Till human voices call us, and we come.

Parlor Piece

By John Crowe Ransom's Cat

—I am a pussycat in a gray coat slinking
Across the living room. Your ears are small
And do not hear my footpads softly fall
In all the racket of your cage-bell's clinking
And chirps and cheeps of your annoying tune;
But I will have my pretty birdie soon,
I am a pussycat in a gray coat slinking.

—You are a parakeet in a cage singing
With nothing on your mind, not even that
Gray cat who tiptoes like an acrobat
Along the shelf. But then you hear the creak
As I release the cage door, and you shriek.
You are a parakeet in heaven singing.

Calico Cat's

by e. e. cummings's cat

Calico Cat's
declawed
        who used to
        rip the silkysoft Persian

                        carpet
and shred onetwothreefourfive chipmunksjustlikethat

                                Jesus

there was a handsome puss

                    and what I want to know is
how would you like your nails pulled out
Mister Vet

From CAT YEARS
by Ogden Nash's Cat

Paradox

I wonder why no human ever seems to catch on
That things that aren't forbidden are no fun to scratch on.

One of Nine Million Reasons Why Cats Are Superior to Dogs

The next time you put on your waterproof togs
And venture outside while it rains us and dogs,
Ask which you'd rather have land on your noodle:
A cute little cat or a ninety-pound poodle?

A Matter of Perspective

I know dead mice aren't very nice
When dropped right at your feet;
You no doubt wish you could entice
Your cat to be discreet.

But as you view the things I slew,
Just think what luck you've got:
Your basement's free of caribou,
And I'm no ocelot.

Do Not Go Peaceable to That Damn Vet

by Dylan Thomas's Cat

Do not go peaceable to that damn vet,
A cat can always tell a trip is due,
Hide, hide, when your appointment time is set.

Wise cats who watched, and learned the alphabet,
And never let men know how much they knew,
Do not go peaceable to that damn vet.

Young cats who want to keep their claws to whet
On sofa legs, and save their privates, too,
Hide, hide, when your appointment time is set.

Sick cats, poor things, whose stomachs are upset,
But hate to eat some evil-smelling goo,
Do not go peaceable to that damn vet.

Old cats who have no wish to sleep just yet,
And plan to live another life or two,
Hide, hide, when your appointment time is set.

And though your human sweetly calls his pet,
Or rants and raves until his face is blue,
Do not go peaceable to that damn vet,
Hide, hide, when your appointment time is set.

Meowl

by Allen Ginsberg's Cat

I saw the best kittens of my litter abandoned by humans,
　　feral delirious rabid,

propelling themselves through the calico weeds in over-
　　grown railyards, searching for a catnip hit,

silverwhiskered hipcats purring in blissful herbal intoxi-
　　cation leaping to bat the hard white moon-ball
　　bouncing in the black-top sky,

who crossed the paths of superstitious pedestrians and
　　strolled with ominous nonchalance under window-
　　washers' ladders,

who cowered in the window of the A.S.P.C.A. shelter
　　hoping that the lunatic in the loden green loungewear
　　would adopt the paranoid parrot instead,

who ran through the subway tunnels pursued by herds
　　of rats as big as broncos rhinos hippos, enormous ar-
　　mored rodents hammering along the knife-bright rails
　　on horny hooves,

who were chased by stir-crazy dogs in Central Park and
　　clambered up Cleopatra's Needle using the edges of
　　the smog-softened hieroglyphs as paw-holds and sat
　　laughing on the pointed peak at the impotent mutts
　　below,

who whined and shrieked like car alarms in the brown-
stone gardens of uptown matrons until they put out
the leftover gravlax appetizers in a Spode china dish,
who fell off a ledge of the Plaza Hotel trying to evade
the house dick after browsing on room service trays
and landed on little cat feet ten stories down this is a
true story and walked away totally intact, and didn't
even rate a photo in the *Post* let alone Animal of the
Year on the cover of *Time* magazine,
who caught and killed and actually ate a pigeon in Her-
ald Square that tasted of rust & grease & pizza crusts &
bus exhaust,
who bit the animal control officer on the ankle and
dived into a storm drain and thereby narrowly
avoided ending up in a lab cage at Brookhaven wear-
ing a plutonium flea collar,
who slipped into an exhibit of dadaist art in a gallery in
Greenwich Village and dined on cheese cubes and
cheap Chablis for a week until the artist showed up
and petulantly declared that although the jar of water
beetles and the box turtle with the padlock on its foot
were part of his aesthetic conception, the cat most
definitely was not,

who were adopted by Mafiosi while hanging around in
   an alley next to the Fulton Fish Market and lived
   for a month in an overdecorated duplex on Queens
   Boulevard until someone found the decapitated corpse
   in the trunk of an Oldsmobile at Newark Airport,
   and the cops came, and the lasagna ran out,

who lived happily for one whole year in a mouse-
   bountiful bookstore on Broadway which one blown
   Monday was bought by Moloch Inc. a national chain
   which put up metal detectors and Garfield posters and
   hired an exterminator,

who paused halfway across the Brooklyn Bridge's vibrat-
   ing wire-woven web looking for the iron spiders, and
   saw instead a madman make a clumsy human jump
   into the oily Lethe's filthy Bronxward flow, and
   thought cats would never do that what with their
   allotted span of no score and 10 to 15 years, not
   exactly a life sentence, and all that slimy fur to clean
   and dry if they failed,

who saw a fifty-foot Kodak kitten on a billboard in
   Times Square and hallucinated a King Kong Kitty
   stroll through midtown Manhattan pulverizing multi-
   tudes with two-ton paws,

and who afterward bounded through the sour streets
   inspired by a vision of the power of the meow the
   holy vowels the ultimate animal mantra the lone phe-
   nomenal feline diphthong,

to repeat the one sound song shout pure mysterious yell
containing all words phrases speeches novels pam-
phlets leaflets ballads epics textbooks archives monu-
mental columned bibliographies filled with infinite
alphabets of unfathomable meaning,

the burned-out stray and bebop misfit cat, unowned,
who beat skulls numb with metered feet and cried
out loud what cats have said before and still have yet
to say in all the eons after death,

and reappeared nine lives later in the tinsel socks of fame
in the blazing arc-light glare of the tube and trum-
peted America's rampant love of dear sweet pussy in
a Hail to the Chief Cat saxophone caterwaul that
scattered the dogwalkers down to the last pooper-
scooper,

with the indigestible furball of the poem in the heart
coughed up out of their own bodies onto the absolute
center of the immaculate carpet of life.